The Guide to OneNote

How to Use OneNote Effectively and Efficiently

Chapter 1. Getting Started and Features

With our lives going a million miles a minute, it's easy to forget things. The big things are important, but what about all the little things that normally get passed by the wayside? It's no longer realistic to expect notebooks to be stashed away in backpacks and briefcases to be brought out when an idea hits. Instead, smartphones, tablets, netbooks, laptops, and desktop computers surround us every waking minute of the day, begging to store everything you want to remember in the cloud. Forget your notes at home? No worries, they're right here on this phone app!

You could spend days searching for the perfect app or piece of software that will meet all of your needs, but there's one program that stands above the rest and it's been hiding right under your nose the whole time. Enter Microsoft OneNote. This note-taking wonder is packaged with MS Office along with Word, PowerPoint, and Excel. Not only that, it's free for download at http://www.onenote.com/ and it can be downloaded on any platform. If you use Microsoft programs regularly, you will likely feel right at home. Ready to give it a try? This chapter explains how to get started taking notes with OneNote.

Creating Notebooks, Sections, and Pages

First we need to make a new notebook (1.1). You have a few choices on where to save your new notebook, but the default will be on your local hard drive. If you have a OneDrive (formerly SkyDrive) account, it will prompt you to log-in and you can save it there and access it on any other device you can access SkyDrive on. It's recommended to name the notebook something

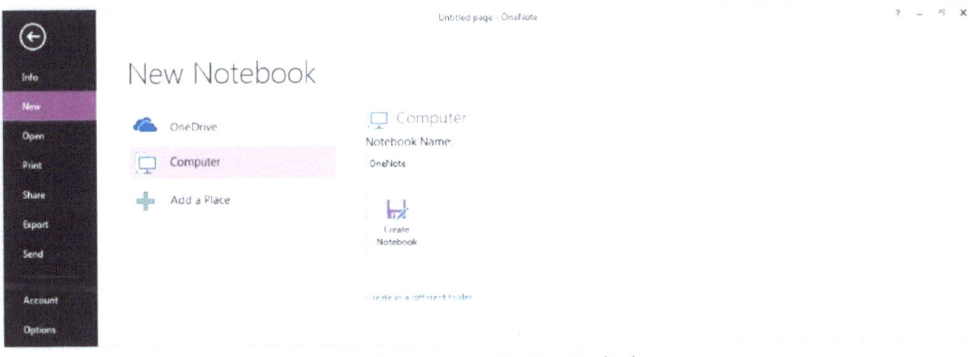

1.1: Creating a new OneNote Notebook.

general because your new notebook can save a *lot* of information!

Congrats! You now own a digital notebook. All that space available might seem a little overwhelming at first because OneNote doesn't limit you to 8.5" x 11" pages. Let's check out all the features before getting started (1.2).

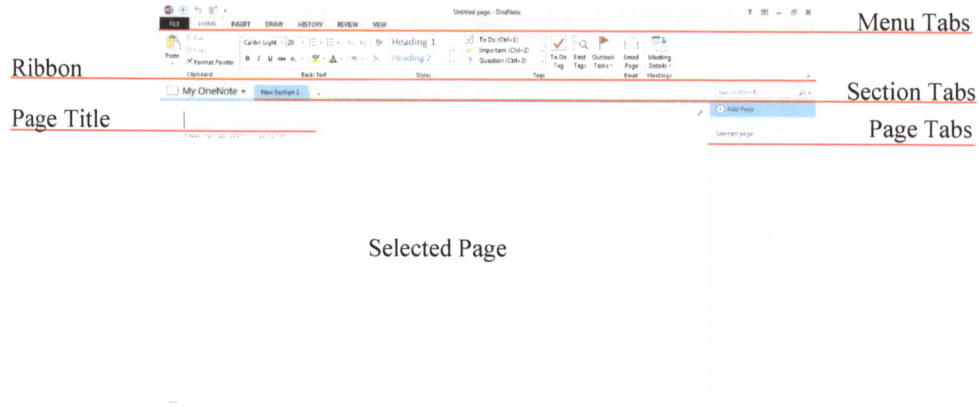

Ribbon

Page Title

Menu Tabs

Section Tabs

Page Tabs

Selected Page

1.2: Features of the OneNote program and page.

In summary, each Menu Tab has a respective Ribbon that consists of groups of tools. This layout is consistent for other Microsoft programs. Once you get past the Ribbon, the name of your notebook is shown to the right of an icon of an open notebook. Clicking on the notebook name will open a list where you can create new notebooks and view/open other notebooks you've created.

To the right of the notebook name are the Section Tabs (1.2). Remember how you used to buy dividers for your binder to keep notes organized by subject? That's what Section Tabs do. Create as many as you like! Your notebook starts with a tab called "New Section 1". Double click the default to rename the section.

Now you're to where the real action happens, the pages! Each page starts blank with the exception of a horizontal line followed by the date and time the page was created (1.3). Put your cursor above that line and give your page a name. You might have noticed that on renaming the page, the Page Tab on the very right of your screen also changed. This window is where the title of all your pages will show as you start populating your section.

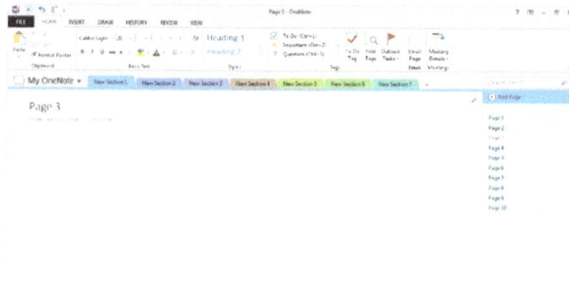

If you already knew how to populate your sections, it probably looks something like this. If not, no worries, it will be soon enough!

Now that you know how to get started, the next chapter will show you what kind of tools you can leverage to make your notes most effective. Feel free to take some notes so you can try out all these cool features.

1.3: Creating new sections and pages.

Shortcuts

OneNote has many shortcuts built in to save you time while writing your notes. These may include icons, keyboard shortcuts, and right-click menus.

Common Icons

OneNote has many icons that indicate a shortcut or action. In addition to the ones listed below, all of the tools have associated icons, so seeing any of those means the icon will do what its associated tool does.

Diagonal Double-arrow icon: Symbolizes the ability to switch to full page view and lets you return back to normal view.

Ellipses icon: Symbolizes that an item may be clicked and dragged (e.g., note groups and docked windows) or that there are more options to choose from on a menu item.

Plus icon: Lets you know that you can add new items. Typically for adding new Notebooks, Sections, and Pages.

Down Arrow icon: Found below, or next to, tools to indicate that a drop down menu will open to give you more options.

More Arrow icon: Usually on list boxes and indicates that there are more options.

Keyboard Shortcuts

There are keyboard shortcuts for most actions. The most common ones are Undo (CTRL + Z), Copy (CTRL + C), Paste (CTRL + V), and Cut (CTRL + X). The best way to learn the shortcuts for your most used tools is to mouse-over the tool for its tool-tip (1.4). If the tool has an associated keyboard shortcut, it will be in bold listed directly to the right of the tool's name.

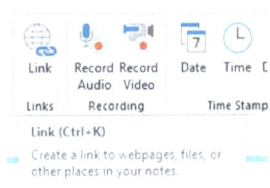

1.4: A tooltip shown on mouse-over of Link tool.

Right-click Menus

Right clicking on your notes opens up a window with icons and a dropdown menu. The options that appear in both the window and menu depend on the type of material in your notes.

Right-clicking on typed notes will open up a small font and tag option window and a drop down menu for copying, pasting, linking, looking up words, and translations (1.5).

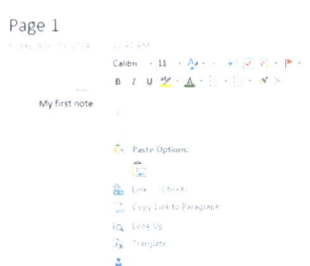

1.5: Right-click menu for typed text.

On the other hand, selecting and right-clicking on drawn, handwritten notes opens up a small window for adding to Outlook tasks, tagging, changing pen properties, or deleting the selection (1.6). The dropdown menu for drawings also has options for cutting and copying, but in addition has options for rotating and ink-related options. Treat Selected Ink As lets you tell the program if your ink is a drawing or handwriting. If you choose handwriting, the option to turn that Ink to Text can be selected. Both handwriting and drawings can select the Ink to Math tool. Both tools will be covered in Chapter 2.

1.6: Right-click menu for selected drawings or handwritten text.

Right-clicking on other items and tools in OneNote can show you commonly used options relevant to the selection or item.

Search

An avid note-taker is likely to get lost in their notes, but luckily all notes are searchable! The search bar is located right above the Page list sidebar, but it lets you know the keyboard shortcut so that you can search without having to go over to the bar (1.7). The keyboard shortcut is useful when you are typing and realize you might have already taken notes on a specific subject. Simply select a word or phrase and press CTRL + E and a search will automatically run.

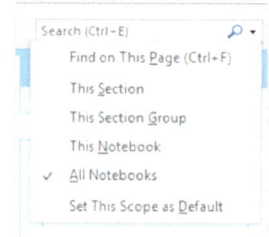

1.7: The search bar and its dropdown menu.

Chapter 2. All about Ribbons

Knowing what kind of tools hidden in each of the ribbons right from the start will make your note-taking much easier. But first, it's important to know that as a MS Office program, it has the ability to communicate with the other Office programs. While we will see these integration tools in the ribbons, they might also be hidden in the ribbons of Word and PowerPoint. We'll go over those in a later chapter.

Home

Many of the tools in the Home ribbon might be familiar to you. The Clipboard, Basic Text, and Styles groups are the usual suspects in all Microsoft programs and work exactly the same. To the right of the Styles group, you'll start with the new stuff.

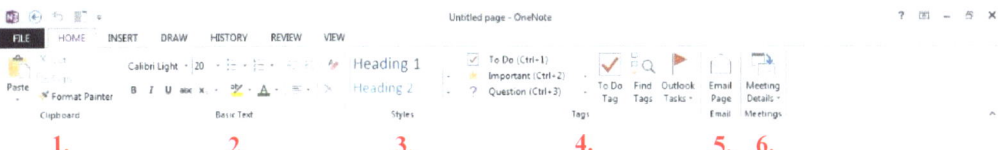

1.   2.   3.   4.   5.   6.

1. Clipboard Group

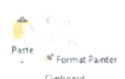

Paste, Cut, and Copy: The usual buttons common to all Microsoft programs.

Format Painter: Also a usual tool, it lets you take formatting from one item in the document and "paint" it on other items in the document.

2. Basic Text Group

Formatting: All of these basic formatting options like font type and size, bulleted lists, and background color are nothing new and will not be covered here.

3. Styles Group

Styles list box: This tool has options similar to the Styles group in MS Word, but with a smaller number of choices. Many different headings can be selected, as well as the page title style, citation, quote, code, and normal styles.

4. Tags Group

Tag Box: This is a list box of tags that you can scroll through.
Clicking the More arrow will cause the entire list of available tags to show. There are many tags to choose from, like: Critical, Remember for blog, and Idea. You can even customize tags by creating new ones based on a chosen tag or by modifying an existing tag.

<u>To Do Tag:</u> The first tag in the list box. Use this tag to indicate a "to do" item which can be checked on completion.

<u>Find Tags:</u> Use this tool to search for tags in your notes. It comes in handy especially if you use a lot of tags.

<u>Outlook Tasks (2.1):</u> If you use Outlook for your email and to keep track of tasks, this tool is helpful if you want to add tasks to Outlook while taking notes in OneNote or vice versa.

2.1: Creating an Outlook Task in OneNote (left) and its appearance in Outlook (right).

5. Email Group

<u>Email Page:</u> As the title suggests, this tool launches Outlook using your default email address and inserts your current notes page into the new message. All you have to do is type in the email address of the person you want to give the page to and click send!

6. Meetings Group

<u>Meeting Details:</u> This tool also uses Outlook. Clicking it brings up a list of meetings for the current day from your Outlook Calendar. You can also go through past or future meetings. Once the correct meeting is selected, OneNote will pull out all the details and attach them to your notes.

Insert

This ribbon contains many tools that will allow you to customize your notes by attaching as much external content as you desire. Many are self-explanatory and similar to those in the Word and PowerPoint Insert Ribbons and will be covered only briefly.

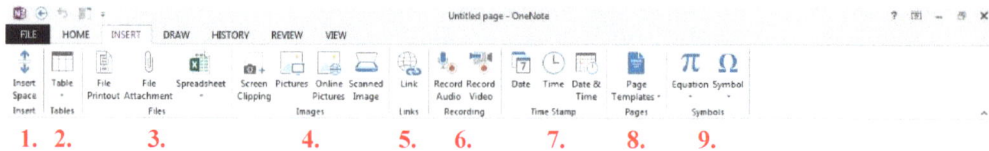

1. Insert Group

Insert Space (2.2): This tool lets you create a space as large as you want. Simply select the tool and then click and drag where you want the space to go. Insert Space is useful if you find you need some extra space to include additional information like drawings or

2.2: Inserting a space between notes with the Insert Space tool.

pictures.

2. Tables Group

Tables: Create a table in your notes to insert information in a more orderly format. Selecting this tool will allow you to create a table with the number of cells you indicate on the drop-down menu, draw your own table, or make a table with an Excel spreadsheet. If you do decide to make your own table, a new Table Tools Layout ribbon appears with options for it. You can even sort your table or convert it to an Excel spreadsheet if you'd like.

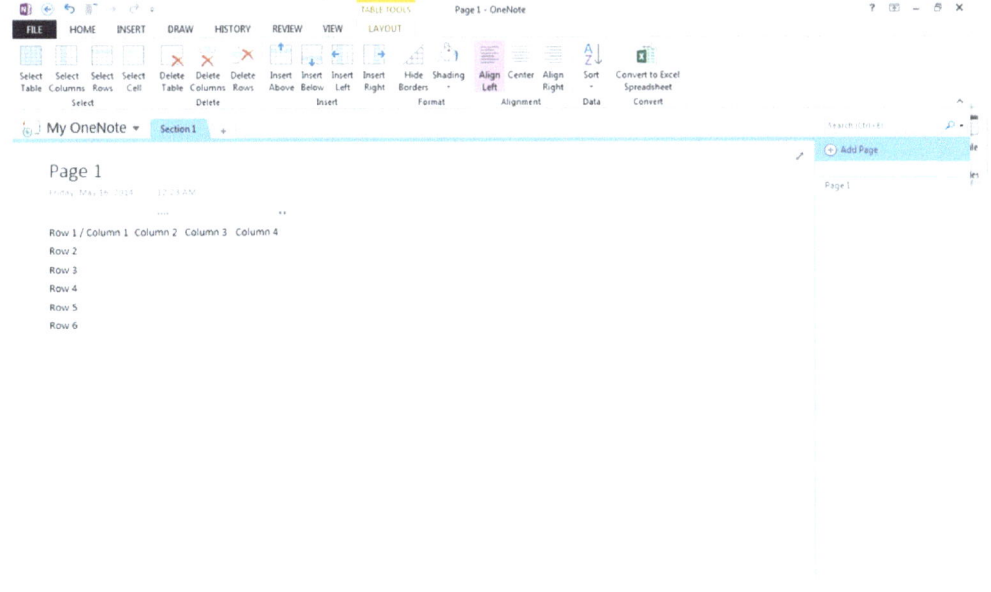

2.3: Creating a table in OneNote and the layout option ribbon that appears.

3. Files Group

<u>File Printout:</u> What this tool does is prompt you to choose a file from your computer which it will then create a "printout" of. It inserts a link to the file and the actual file into your notes in a format that looks like a printed or scanned image of the document. This "printout" is not able to be edited, but you can click on the link to open the original file for editing. Note: by default you may only use File Printout with Microsoft Office Program files.

<u>File Attachment:</u> Similar to File Printout, File Attachment prompts you to select a document to attach to your notes. However, there are no limitations to the type of file you can attach. This tool only provides an icon of the type and name of the document you have attached and does not attach a printout of the document as well.

<u>Spreadsheet (2.3):</u> Clicking this tool gives you two options: Existing Excel Spreadsheet and New Excel Spreadsheet. Choosing Existing Excel Spreadsheet will prompt you to choose the Excel file from your computer while New Excel Spreadsheet will insert a small spreadsheet into your notes. Choosing New Excel Spreadsheet is the same in this tool and the Tables tool.

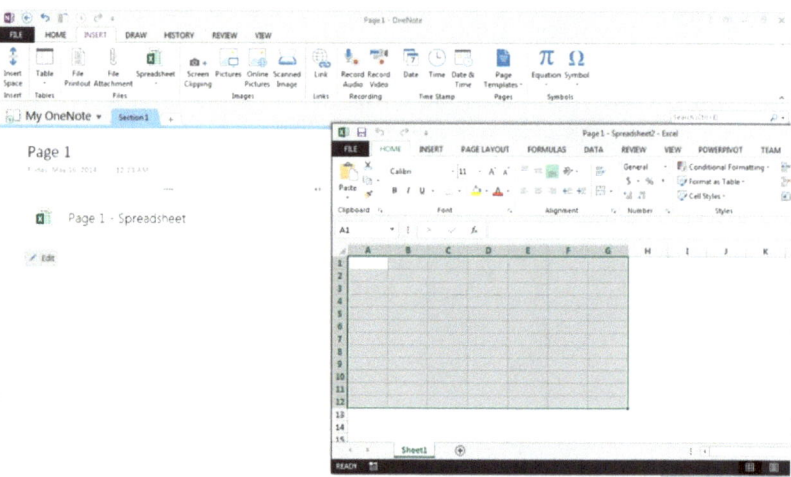

2.4: Using the Spreadsheet tool to insert a new spreadsheet and open a new Excel file associated to your notes.

4. Images Group

<u>Screen Clipping:</u> This brings up the most recently viewed screen where a clipping can then be taken and inserted into notes. Be sure to have open the

page you want to take a clipping of before going back to OneNote because once this tool has been chosen it will not let you change the screen to be clipped.

Pictures: As with all other programs with this tool, it opens the computer's file browser so an image can be selected and inserted into notes.

Online Pictures (2.4): Clicking this will open a window where you have a few options: Office.com Clip Art, Bing Image Search, your OneDrive account, Facebook, or Flickr. If you chose Facebook or Flickr, it will prompt you to enter in your account information so it can access your photos.

2.5: The Insert Pictures window that opens on selecting the Online Pictures tool.

Scanned Image: Choosing Scanned Image will open up the program your computer has associated with an attached scanner so that you may scan in a document or photo to be inserted into the notes.

5. Links Group

Link: When writing notes, you might have information from external websites or from within other notes you have taken. That's when the Link tool may be used. To link, highlight the text you want to link and then click the Link tool. The "Text to display" will automatically be the highlighted text. Then you can copy and paste a link, search the internet (it will use your default browser), search your computer to link a file, or you can even search through your other notebooks and notes.

6. Recording Group

Record Audio (2.5): Be ready when choosing this tool! On click three things happen, the toolbar changes to an audio recording studio, it automatically begin recording audio, and an icon of a .WAV file named after the page will be inserted into your notes. This comes in handy if you are an auditory learner or you want to speak your thoughts to be typed at a later date. For students, Record Audio is useful to record lectures to listen to later.

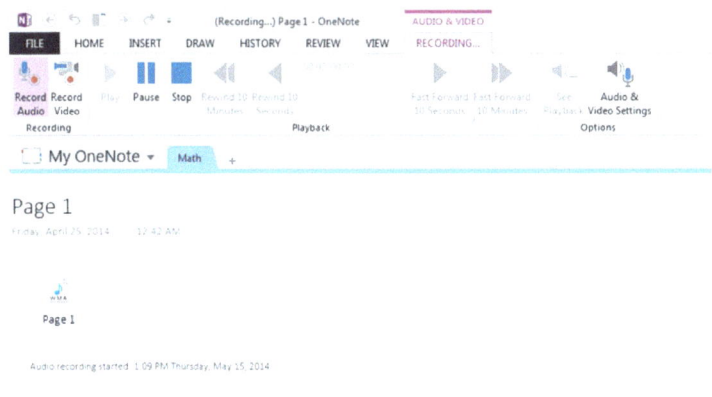

2.6: Change in the ribbon and additions to a page when using the Record Audio tool.

Record Video: Extremely similar to Record Audio, Record Video simply takes video from your computer's webcam.

7. Time Stamp Group

Date: Clicking Date will simply enter in the current date.

Time: Similarly, Time will enter in your current time.

Date & Time: This tool will enter in both today's date and time.

8. Pages Group

Page Templates (2.6): Page Templates can be a huge time saver if you do anything requiring a common format, such as taking notes every day for college classes. Clicking the Page Templates tool will open a drop down menu where you can choose from a variety of template types. Note: choosing a template will make a new page. The last option, Page Templates…, will open up a sidebar that breaks down each template group into a list of templates to choose from.

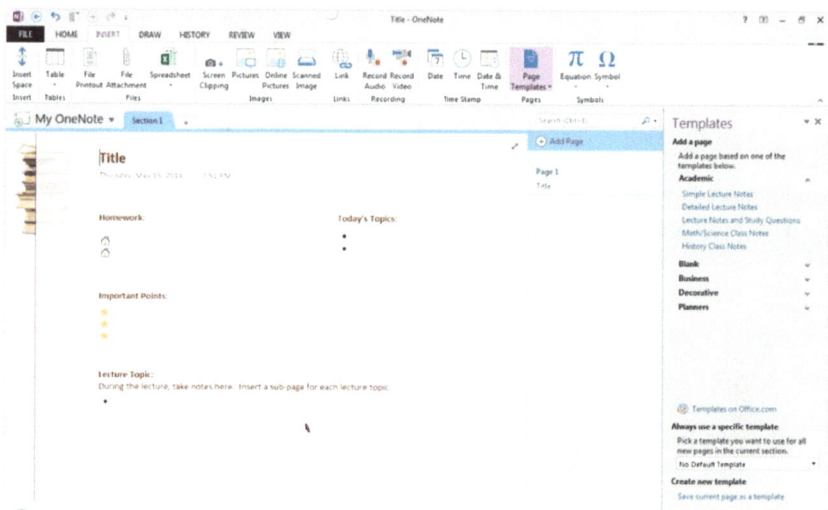

2.7: Using the "Detailed Lecture Notes" template.

The example template shown above is "Detailed Lecture Notes". It includes homework tags, bullet points for the topics covered during the class, tags for important points of the lecture, and even tips for making a new sub-page for each lecture topic covered.

9. Symbols Group

Equation (2.7): With this tool you have a variety of common math equations to choose from such as the area of a circle and the Pythagorean Theorem. They will look like this: $A = \text{Ï}\in r^2$ or $a^2 + b^2 = c^2$, respectively. Once you're working with the Equation tool,

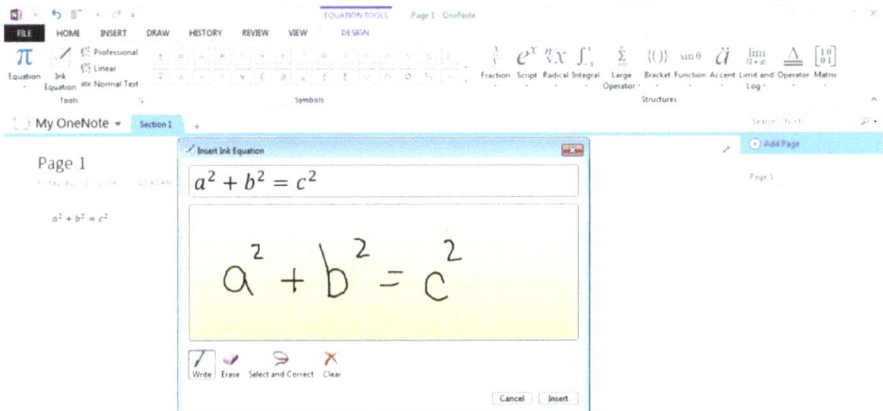

you

2.8: The Equation Tools Design ribbon and ability to handwrite equations.

have many options to choose from to either customize an equation or create new equations. Each of the Equation Tools in the Design Tab can take some getting used to, but come in handy for anything needing easily-readable equations. In addition, you can write equations by hand or with your mouse and OneNote will create typed equations for you!

Symbol: Clicking the Symbols tool opens a drop-down box of common and recently used symbols as well as the ability to choose from a large variety of additional symbols.

Draw

The Draw ribbon is great for making your notes stand out by pointing out information, drawing diagrams, or highlighting PDFs.

1. Tools group

Type: The default way of taking notes is by typing them, so this should be selected

unless you're taking notes a different way. Remember to reselect this option when you want to return to typing your notes.

Lasso Select: This tool allows you to select things by drawing around them and makes an easier alternative to holding down the Shift key and clicking on items to select things. After selection, you may drag the items around the screen to make your notes better organized.

Panning Hand: The panning hand allows you to click and drag to pan to another part of your page, which is particularly helpful if your page(s) are very long and it becomes too much hassle scrolling through.

Eraser: Selecting the Eraser tool opens a dropdown menu so that you can choose the size of the eraser you would like. Then simply click and drag over shapes and/or drawings to erase. You can also use the Stroke Eraser which lets you erase entire stroke marks made by the pen and highlighter tools. Note: Eraser does not erase type, only drawings and shapes.

Drawing tool list box (2.8): The default list box has a few different choices of pen color, thicknesses, and highlighter colors. Opening the dropdown menu gives you even more choices of sizes and colors. Use the Pen Mode to indicate what you will be using the drawing tools for: handwriting and drawing, drawing only, or handwriting only. Another option is to use the pen as a pointer. What this does is allow you to draw an arrow to parts of your notes that will disappear after a short period of time. This is useful if your notes are part of a presentation or you are

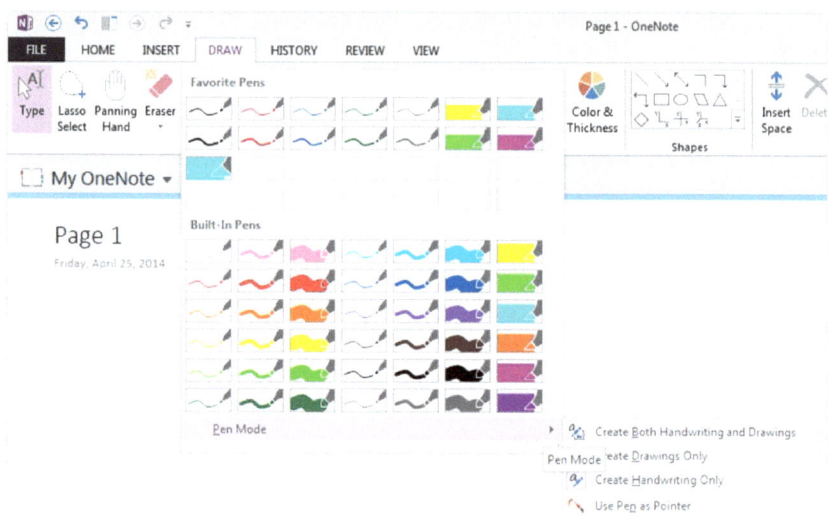

2.9: Dropdown menus and options associated with the Draw list box.

explaining your notes to a colleague or fellow student.

Color & Thickness: easily customize pens and highlighters to the color and thickness you want

2. Shapes Group:

Shapes: Draw basic lines, shapes, and even graph axes. You can choose to enter "Drawing Mode" if you will be using the drawing tools and not typed text for long period of time. This takes away the possibility of accidently clicking on a text box and switching functions. If you're drawing shapes, you can snap them to the grid for a nicer layout.

3. Edit Group

Insert Space: This is the same tool from the Insert Tab, Insert Space tool. Click and drag to create a space between your notes.

Delete: Clicking this simply deletes drawings, highlighted text, or selected note boxes.

Arrange: Arrange your drawings into layers on the page. That is, bring a specific drawing to the front or send it backwards in related to other drawings on the page.

Rotate: Rotate your drawing or shape in many different directions or you can choose to flip it.

4. Convert Group

Ink to Text: If you're taking notes on a touch screen during a class or meeting, select the hand-written notes and then click on the Ink to Text tool. It will convert your handwriting into typed notes instantly. However, if your notes are messy it may have trouble deciphering them.

Ink to Math: Similar to Ink to Text, but instead it will convert handwritten math formulas into nicely organized equations.

History

The History ribbon is useful when a notebook is being shared between two or more people, but is also useful for private content only accessible by you between a number of devices.

1. Unread Group

Next Unread: If there are any unread notes in your notebook, scroll through them with this tool.

Mark as Read: The Mark as Read group allows you to mark notes as read or unread as needed. For example, if your notebook is only shared between two of your personal devices, you might want to mark the notes you took on one other device as read when you open them on one another device. You might also want to mark read notes as unread notes if you feel you need to go over them again later.

2. Authors Group

Recent Edits: Choosing this tool opens a drop down menu that lets you choose a view of recent edits to the notebook by you or anyone else who may have access. A sidebar will open in which you may search for other recent edits and filter the results.

Find by Author: If many different people have access to a notebook, which may be the case for a shared office project, you may search for edits made by one person. This too opens up the Search Results sidebar where you can filter results.

Hide Authors: If many people are editing the same notes page it can get confusing. Click the Hide Authors tool to hide the author name that shows up next to the edits.

3. History Group

Page Versions: Click this and on choosing Page Versions from the drop down menu, all previous versions of your page will be shown beneath the pages' name. Click to view them and a yellow bar pops up warning you that this is an older version. To restore a previous version all you have to do is click that yellow bar and choose "Restore Version". Other options allow you to delete the version, copy it to a new page, and delete all pages in the section and/or notebook.

Notebook Recycle Bin: This is where all of the deleted pages, sections, and notebooks go to. Again, you may restore anything listed by clicking on the yellow bar that pops up. Note: old versions are permanently deleted after 60 days.

Review

The Review ribbon doesn't have many options, but 4 out of 7 of them should be familiar to you. Spelling, Thesaurus, Translate, and Language are all tools found in the other MS Office Programs. You might have seen the Research tool as well depending on which programs you frequent because surprisingly, it's not to be seen in Word.

1. Spelling Group

Spelling: The normal spellchecker tool.

Research: Even if you have never seen or used the Research tool, it is very intuitive. Clicking it will bring up a sidebar that lets you conduct searches using sources in the dropdown menu (default is Bing search). If you highlight text before clicking on the tool, it will automatically insert the highlighted text into the search bar.

Thesaurus: Selecting the Thesaurus tool opens a sidebar where you can enter in a word to check for synonyms. Alternatively, you can highlight text and then click the tool and it will automatically search for synonyms.

2. Language Group

Translate: The Translate tool gives you the ability to translate your notes into another language. You can choose the language you want your notes to be translated to by going to the option at the bottom of the drop down menu.

Language: Similarly, the Language tool lets you choose what language you want OneNote to proof (spellcheck) your notes with and the language to use when translating handwritten notes to text.

3. Section Group

Password: This tool allows you to password protect things. More specifically, it will bring up a sidebar where you can create a password to secure the currently selected section tab. Please be sure to read the instructions though, as some functions are not allowed. For instance, information contained within a protected section is unsearchable and must first be unlocked.

4. Notes Group

Linked Notes: The last tool in this ribbon, Linked Notes, is used while the page is docked to the desktop. Its purpose is to attach notes to the window currently open other than OneNote. This is particularly useful if you're taking notes on PDF documents or digital books.

View

This ribbon lets you customize your note-taking experience with a variety of different options. For instance, you can reduce distractions or allow split-screen. You can also make your digital notebook appear similar to a traditional printed notebook. Here, make the notebook comfortable.

1. Views Group

Normal View: This is the default view and because of this, the tool is highlighted in purple.

Full Page View (2.9): Clicking this will bring you into full page view. This removes all tabs, ribbons, and sidebars. Think of it as a "no distraction" view. Return to normal view by clicking the double-sided, diagonal arrows on the top right corner of the screen.

2.10: How a page looks in Full Page View.

Dock to Desktop: This view is perfect when your notes are based on information taken from the web or another program. Dock to Desktop docks the current notes page to the side or bottom of your computer screen so that you may take notes while viewing another window simultaneously. Note: Click and drag the ellipses (…) symbol at the top of the docked notes page to change where it docks on your screen. Additionally, this view links the notes taken to whatever window it is that you have open while typing the notes. The first time docking notes, OneNote will warn you that it is doing this. You may stop taking linked notes or go to the linked notes options by clicking on the link icon on the top right hand side of the notes page. Similar to Full Page View, click on the double-sided, diagonal arrows on the top right corner of the screen to return to normal view.

2. Page Setup Group

Page Color: Change the color of your pages using this tool. All colors are a light pastel so they don't distract your writing.

Rule Lines (2.10): Select this tool to open a dropdown menu that will let you give your page rule lines and make the page feel like a real notebook. Choose from wide rule, college rule, small grid, large grid, and others. If there are rule lines on the page, you can change their color. You can also decide if you want to set rule lines as a default for all new pages opened.

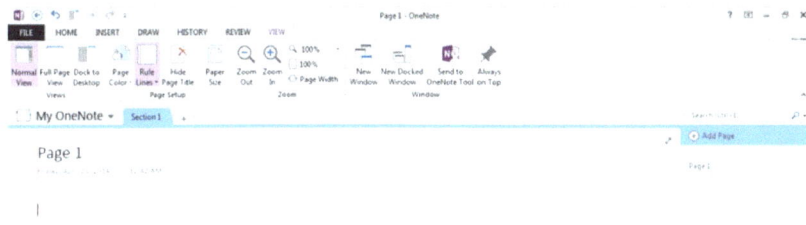

Hide Page Title: Clicking this tool simply removes the title, date, and time from the page. Click again to bring it all back.

Paper Size: The Paper Size tool opens a sidebar where you can choose from a standard paper size or enter in a specific height and width. For printing purposes, you may also indicate print margins. You may also save your paper size as a template.

3. Zoom Group

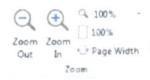

Zoom Out: This tool makes your page zoom out so you can see more of the notes you have entered.

Zoom In: In contrast, this tool zooms in your page so you can look at the finer details of certain notes.

Page Width: Clicking this will zoom your page to the full width of all notes taken. For instance, if your page is wider than it is long, this tool will zoom your notes to where you can see all notes spanning the entire width of the page.

4. Window Group

New Window: This tool opens up a new window identical to the current OneNote window, which includes notes and all. You might use this if you want to take notes on multiple pages at once or create two versions of the same page. Remember that these versions can be viewed with the History tab.

New Docked Window: This tool also opens up a new window identical to the current window only the new window will be docked to your desktop and take linked notes.

Send to OneNote Tool (2.12): One of the most useful tools is Send to OneNote. By default this window opens when OneNote starts. What it does is give you the ability to take

2.13: The Send to OneNote Tool.

screen clippings, insert a printout of a document, and create new quick notes to put into OneNote. We have already covered screen clippings and printouts, but

2.12: The quick notes window.

not quick notes. Quick notes opens up a notepad style window where you can easily type notes on the go (2.11). On exit of the window, a pop-up will let you know where they were saved: to a special Quick Notes folder which can be found at the bottom of your list of Notebooks.

Always on Top: Clicking this will keep your OneNote window on top of any other window you might have open. While not very useful in full page or normal view, it works well if you need to have OneNote and another window in a split screen situation.

Special Function

Special function ribbons are those that appear only when a relevant item is selected. The items or tools that have their own ribbons have many additional functions that aren't able to fit within a normal ribbon. We have already seen an example of these for Tables (2.3), Audio & Video (2.6), and Equations (2.8).

Chapter 3. Touch Screen Notes

Remember the Draw Ribbon? This is where it really shines. Handwriting your notes and having the ability to draw figures to illustrate or add upon your ideas gives a more authentic note-taking experience despite using a digital interface. The version examined here is OneNote 2013 running on a Windows 8.1 RT tablet, but the full version of OneNote 2013 is also touch-compatible.

The two major differences between the desktop and touch screen versions of OneNote is layout and options. The touch screen version is optimized to a smaller screen, so the layout reacts accordingly and your current page is typically in Full Page View mode. The other difference is that there are no Tabs or Ribbons for your tools. Instead, all the tools are in a fantastic little wheel that keeps out of your way.

Layout

The simple layout makes note-taking a breeze, whether you're typing using an external or on-screen keyboard or taking handwriting notes using your finger or a stylus (3.1).

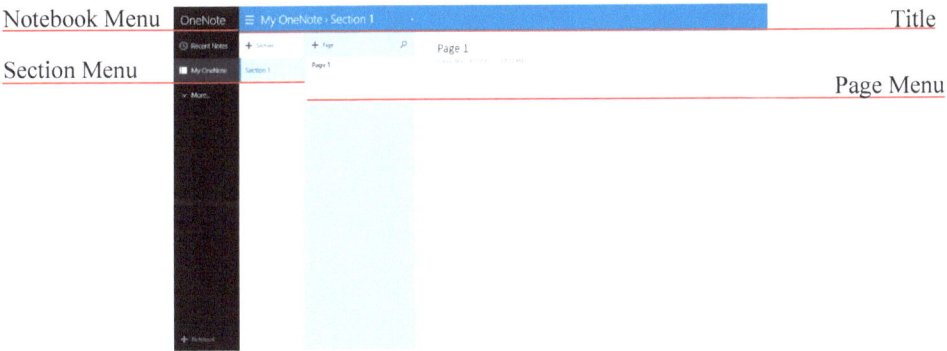

Notebook Menu — Title

Section Menu — Page Menu

3.1: Features of the touch screen version of OneNote.

The full-screen Page doesn't allow for many distractions, so this is a perfect tool to use in even a formal situation.

Radial Menu

The tool wheel, or radial menu, is a touch-friendly option to ribbons in the traditional OneNote program. Luckily the menu is very intuitive. When you tap the screen, three things appear: a blinking cursor, a circle below the cursor, and a circle with a page and an arrow inside (3.2). If you're using the touch screen keyboard, that will also appear.

3.2: Icons that appear when tapping the page screen.

Tapping the circled page icon will make the radial menu appear with all the tools appearing in the style of a clock face (3.3). Now imagine the menu is a pie where each tool has its own slice or section and the surrounding circle is the crust. If the tool's "crust" is dark purple and contains an arrow that means there are more options available for that tool.

3.3: The main radial menu and sub-menus associated with tools having additional options.

The draw icon is one you might use frequently if you are planning on taking notes by hand or will be doing a lot of drawings. On click of the Draw tool, the radial menu disappears and you are left with an icon of a pen and ink at the top right hand corner of the screen, indicating you're in draw mode. Tapping this new icon will open up a radial menu with only drawing-related options (3.4).

 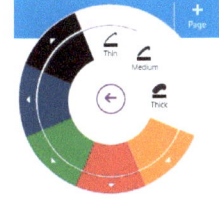

3.4: Drawing menu (left) and color and thickness options for each Pen (right).

As they do with drawing, the menus change based on your activities. Selecting text causes the

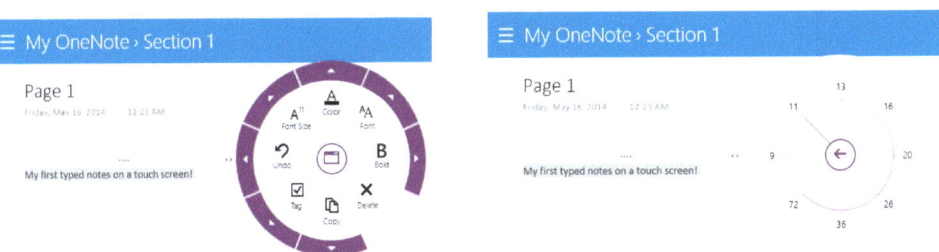

3.5: Font-related options appear on the radial menu when text is selected (left). If Font Size is chosen, the menu turns into a dial that can be turned to increase or decrease the font size.

menu to change to one with all the different font options (3.5).

You may notice that there is no select tool in any of the radial menus, but don't worry. That function is left to the little circle right below the cursor bar. Remember it? Tap on your screen to make it show up, then press your finger or stylus to it and drag around the item(s) you want to select (3.6). Great! The little circle is a Lasso Select tool which we saw in Chapter 2.

3.6: Selecting handwritten text using the cursor's lasso tool.

Chapter 4. Taking Notes

As evidenced by the previous chapters, you really have an unlimited number of ways to not just take notes, but also organize them.

Explicit

Direct note-taking is when you sit down with the explicit intent to write down notes. You might just be writing notes at the end of the day or you might be taking notes during a business meeting. This type of writing benefits from using Normal View or Full Page View to reduce distractions.

Linked

For this type of note-taking you are probably wanting to take notes regarding a specific document and linked notes using the docked screen are your best option (4.1).

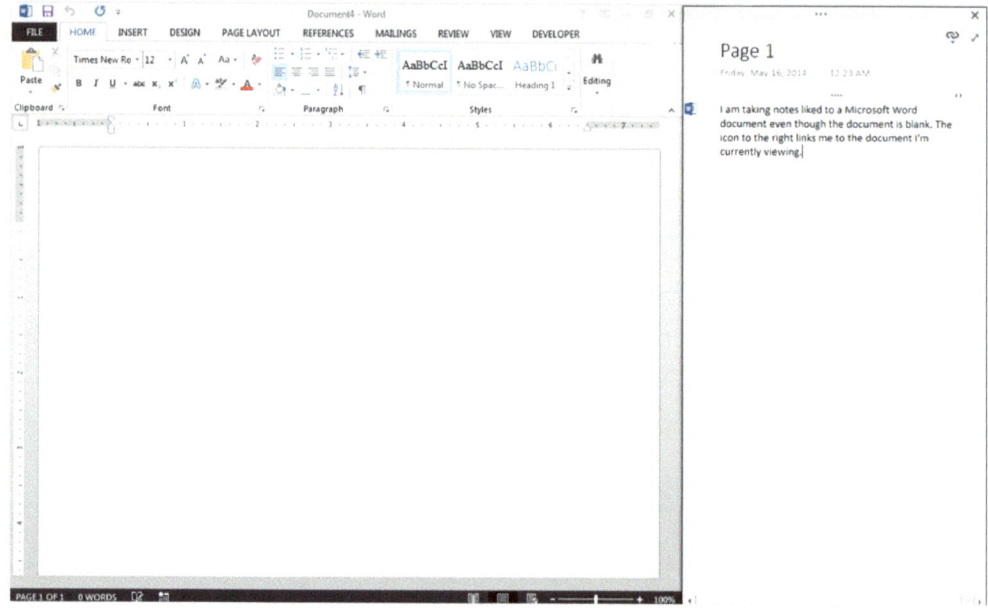

4.1: Linked notes taken while in Dock to Desktop mode.

Indirect

The other note-taking style is indirectly. Perhaps you're browsing the internet and find a recipe you want to save or maybe you're going through your emails and have an event you want to save to your notes. In either case, OneNote is probably minimized on your screen and you'll mostly be using the Send to OneNote tool (4.2).

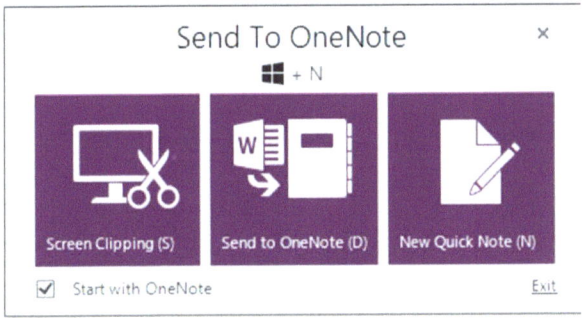

4.2: Send to OneNote Tool.

Chapter 5. Tips, Tricks, and Extras

Looking for even more productivity? There are a few ways to stay on top of your notes with tips/tricks and optional features.

Tips and Tricks

Included here are things that a casual user might not want or need, but are useful for anyone desiring additional functionality and organization.

Microsoft Office Integration

OneNote will show up in some of the other MS Office programs' ribbons.

<u>MS Word:</u> The OneNote icon is found in the Review tab ribbon to activate the Linked Notes tool and dock OneNote to your desktop. This is useful if you have ideas to put in the document, but first they need a good place to go.

<u>MS Excel:</u> While there are no OneNote icons to be found in Excel, the integration ability comes from inserting Excel spreadsheets into your notes.

<u>MS PowerPoint:</u> The OneNote icon is found in the Review tab ribbon to activate the Linked Notes tool and dock OneNote to your desktop. This is useful if you are reviewing a class presentation and would like to take notes on it during or after class.

<u>MS Outlook:</u> By default there is no OneNote icon in Outlook, but you can install an add-in. Go to File > Options > Add-Ins, and at the bottom next to the word "Manage:", click the Go button if COM Add-ins is listed. Check the box next to "OneNote Notes about Outlook Items" and click "OK" (5.1). The Home tab ribbon should now have a OneNote icon in the Move group. Right-clicking a selected email will bring up a dropdown menu that also now includes a OneNote icon.

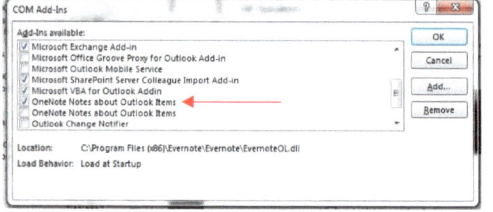

What both icons do is allow you to send the contents of an email to the desired note page. This might be helpful if you are

5.1: Adding OneNote functinality to Outlook.

keeping track of customer complaints or praise for a yearly employee review.

Another OneNote integration with Outlook is the ability to create a page in your notebook dedicated to your contacts. In Outlook, go to the "People" section. Choose a contact and right-click, then choose OneNote. This creates a new page for the contact, their contact information, and an area to take notes. This works well as a Contact Management System if you like to keep track of where you met or how you know people.

Grouping Sections

If you have a lot of sections or sections you want to keep, but keep out of the way, grouping sections is a great tool. Let's say you're a student who just finished your spring 2014 semester

5.2: Right-clicking the section tab area for section options.

classes. First, right-click in the Section Tab area and select New Section Group (5.2).

A new section group will have been created, sitting to the right of the section tabs (5.3).

Now, if the section tabs seen above are for the recently finished semester, they can be dragged and dropped right on top of the "Spring 2014" group, which will move them. Otherwise, section groups can be filled with any sections (5.4).

The way you can tell you're in a section group and not the main page is by the section group's

5.3: A new section group has been added, titled "Spring 2014". Indicated by the red arrow.

5.4: Inside the new section group.

title underneath the Notebook name. The arrow to the right takes you back to the main page.

Copy/Pasting

If you're big into keeping track of where you pull information, OneNote is the way to do it. Copying information from a website and pasting it into OneNote will not only put in the copied

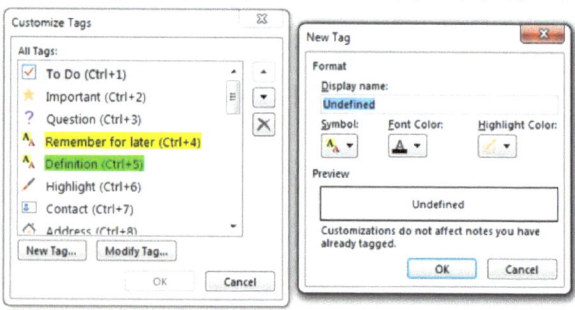

Microsoft OneNote (formerly called Microsoft Office OneNote) is a computer program for free-form information gathering and multi-user collaboration. It gathers users' notes (handwritten or typed), drawings, screen clippings and audio commentaries. Notes can be shared with other OneNote users over the Internet or a network. OneNote is available as a part of the Microsoft Office suite. It is also available as a free stand-alone application for Windows, Mac, Windows RT, Windows Phone, iOS, Android and Symbian.[4] A web-based version of OneNote is provided as part of OneDrive or Office Online and enables users to edit notes via a web browser.

From <http://en.wikipedia.org/wiki/Microsoft_OneNote>

(Ctrl) ▾

5.5: Text copied and pasted from Wikipedia. OneNote's source is found at the bottom of the pasted text in < >.

material, but also the source from which the material came (5.4).

Create Custom Tags

Like tags but need one that means something specific? You can create custom tags to use in your notes (5.6). Click the More arrow on the Tags list box and choose the very last option, Customize

5.6: Creating custom tags.

Tags…

In the window that pops up, choose the New Tag… button. Now customize however you want!

Quick Math Calculations

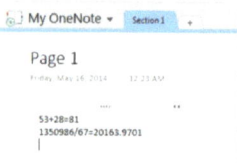

No need to bring out a calculator, OneNote will calculate equations for you (5.7)! All you have to do is type in an equation and follow it with an equal sign.

Convert Images to Text (OCR)

You might have information contained in images, screenshots, and the like. Amazingly, you don't even have to do anything to search the text in images! OneNote automatically makes text in all images searchable. If you simply want to take the text out of an image to use for other purposes, you can also do that. There are programs out there that do just that, but OneNote does it for free. Right-click on the image that you want to take the text out of and choose "Copy Text from Picture". This saves it to your clipboard so you can then paste it elsewhere (5.8). The text that you get may not be perfect, but it does show you what OneNote is looking for during a

5.8: Copying text from an image. Image clipped from wikipedia.org.

search.

Search Audio and Video

Another unique trick is OneNote's ability to decipher words from audio and video. Using audio to record spoken notes is a time saver, but you might want what's being said on paper (or screen in this case). Take audio/video or select an audio/video file in your notes. The Audio & Video

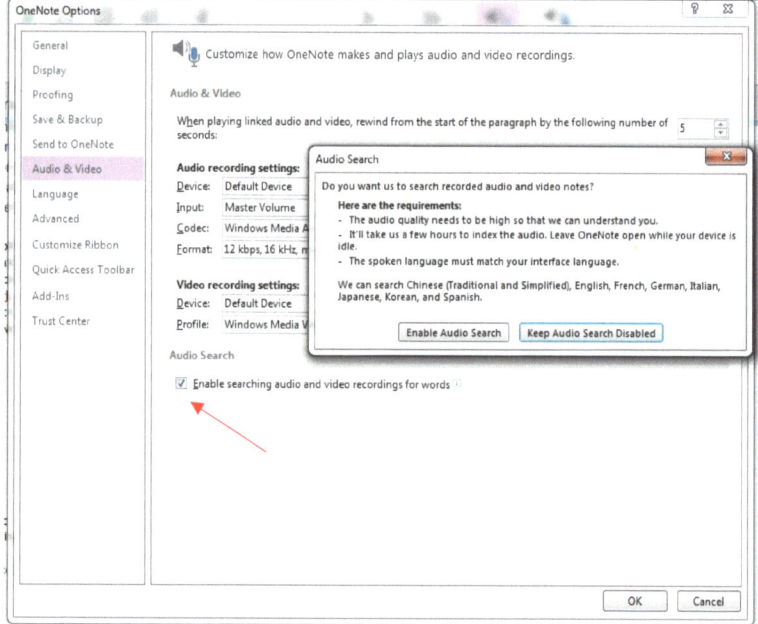

5.9: Enabling audio and video searching.

Playback ribbon will open, which has an Audio & Video Settings tool in the Options group. Clicking that will open the options window. Check the box to enable the program to search your audio and video (5.9). Checking the box will cause another window to pop-up; this one explains the requirements for searching audio and video. It takes some time to work, but once this is enabled, any searches will include multimedia files.

Optional Features

OneNote Online

Going to http://www.onenote.com and logging in with your Microsoft Live account will give you access to all of the Notebooks you have saved into the (5.8).

5.10: OneNote Online Notebook screen. From onenote.com.

And they aren't just read-only versions! Clicking on a Notebook will open up a window that looks very similar to the touch-screen version of OneNote (5.9). Using OneNote online is a life saver if you have internet access, but without your personal computer. All notes from OneNote Online will be synced across your devices.

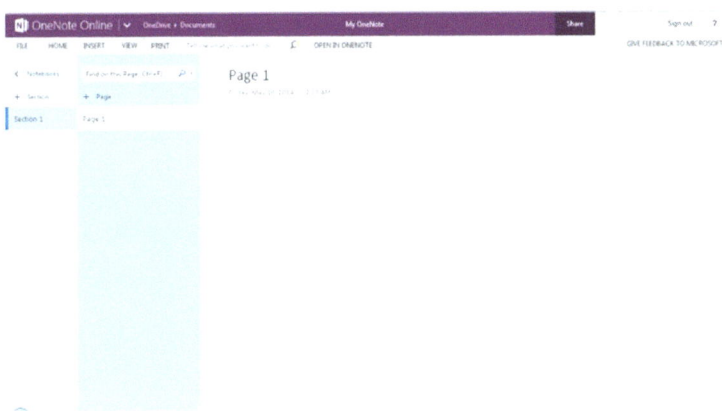

5.11: OneNote Online editor. From onenote.com.

Apps

That's right, there's an app for that! Many sources offer apps with OneNote functionalities for download. Apps are always being developed, so here are links to check for currently downloadable apps.

Microsoft: Check out http://www.onenote.com/apps# to browse through the available apps. Apps offered through Microsoft vary on platform: some are Windows platforms, some for iOS, some for Android, and some for the web. There are even apps for your printer!

Google Chrome Browser: Chrome's app store has a few choices, but the major one lets you go straight to your Microsoft Online OneNote account directly.

Firefox Browser: Firefox has an add-in that lets you clip information from a webpage which is then sent straight to your OneNote notebook.

www.ingramcontent.com/pod-product-compliance
Lightning Source LLC
Chambersburg PA
CBHW050918290526
45792CB00002B/804